The · Life Cycle · Series

The Life Cycle of an

Earthworm

Bobbie Kalman

Crabtree Publishing Company

www.crabtreebooks.com

The Life Cycle Series
A Bobbie Kalman Book

Dedicated by Rose Gowsell
For Treacle, Fringe, and Chet—who have wiggled their way through countless soil heaps

Author and Editor-in-Chief
Bobbie Kalman

Research
Hadley Dyer

Substantive editor
Kathryn Smithyman

Editors
Molly Aloian
Amanda Bishop
Kelley MacAulay
Rebecca Sjonger

Art director
Robert MacGregor

Design
Rose Gowsell

Production coordinator
Heather Fitzpatrick

Photo research
Crystal Foxton

Consultant
Patricia Loesche, Ph.D., Animal Behavior Program,
Department of Psychology, University of Washington

Photographs
Bill Beatty: page 22 (top)
Bruce Coleman Inc.: Kim Taylor: page 14
© Dwight R. Kuhn: pages 8 (bottom), 10, 12, 13, 17, 19, 20, 21, 24, 25, 26,
    27, 28, 30, 31
Robert MacGregor: front cover (earthworms), page 3
Allen Blake Sheldon: page 22 (bottom)
© stephenmcdaniel.com: pages 8 (top), 15, 18
Beverley Van Praagh: page 6
Visuals Unlimited: © Carolina Biological: pages 1, 5 (earthworm), 16;
    © Steve Maslowski: page 9
Other images by Digital Stock

Illustrations:
Barbara Bedell: back cover (except series logo), pages 4 (segmented worm),
7, 8 (magnifying glass), 14 (bottom left and right), 15, 16, 23 (right), 26, 27,
28, 29, 30 (bottom right), 31 (top)
Antoinette "Cookie" Bortolon: front cover, border
Katherine Kantor: pages 11 (soil background), 19 (soil background), 23 (left)
Margaret Amy Reiach: series logo, pages 6, 8 (except magnifying glass), 9,
10, 11 (all except soil background), 12, 13, 14 (top), 17, 19 (earthworm
cocoons), 30 (top left and right), 31 (bottom)
Bonna Rouse: pages 4 (all except segmented worm), 5

Crabtree Publishing Company
www.crabtreebooks.com   1-800-387-7650

Cataloging-in-Publication Data
Kalman, Bobbie.
  The life cycle of an earthworm / Bobbie Kalman.
    p. cm. -- (The life cycle series)
  Includes index.
  ISBN 0-7787-0666-4 (RLB) -- ISBN 0-7787-0696-6 (pbk.)
  1. Earthworms--Juvenile literature. [1. Earthworms. 2. Worms.]
I. Title.
  QL391.A6.K335 2004
  592'.64--dc22
                                2003025586
                                LC

**Published in
the United States**
PMB16A
350 Fifth Ave.
Suite 3308
New York, NY
10118

**Published
in Canada**
616 Welland Ave.,
St. Catharines, Ontario
Canada
L2M 5V6

**Published in the
United Kingdom**
73 Lime Walk
Headington
Oxford
OX3 7AD
United Kingdom

**Published
in Australia**
386 Mt. Alexander Rd.,
Ascot Vale (Melbourne)
VIC 3032

CONTENTS

WONDERFUL WORMS

A worm is an **invertebrate**. Invertebrates are animals that do not have backbones. All worms are **cold-blooded**, which means their body temperatures change as the temperatures of their surroundings change.

roundworm

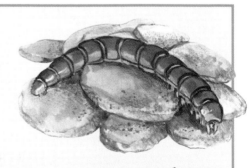

segmented worm

Types of worms

There are thousands of **species**, or types, of worms. Some are so tiny that they can be seen only with a **microscope**. Others are as long as garden hoses! Some worms live in soil. Others live in water. Worms that are **parasites** live on or inside the bodies of other animals. Three major types of worms are roundworms, flatworms, and segmented worms.

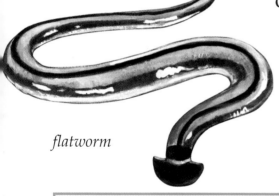

flatworm

Impostors!

inchworm

Some animals are believed to be worms, but they are not worms. A few types of **larvae**, or developing insects, look like worms. Mealworms are beetle larvae. Inchworms are moth larvae.

mealworm

Made of small parts

This book is about the life cycle of an earthworm. Earthworms are segmented worms. The bodies of segmented worms are divided into small parts that are joined together. Scientists call segmented worms **annelids**. Having segmented bodies allows annelids to twist and turn as they move.

Other annelids

Earthworms are not the only type of worms that have segmented bodies. Leeches are also annelids. They live in fresh water. Another group of annelids lives in oceans. They are known as **marine worms**, or sea worms. Bristle worms, feather duster worms, and sea mice are marine worms.

feather duster worm

sea mouse

leech

bristle worm

EARTHWORMS EVERYWHERE

There are more than 2,700 species of earthworms. They can be found almost anywhere in the world except on high mountains and in places with very dry or freezing **climates**.

How long?

Most earthworms are less than twelve inches (30 cm) long. A few species are very large.

They are known as **giant worms**. Two giant earthworm species—the Oregon giant and the giant Palouse—have been known to live in North America. Both grow to about three feet (1 m) long. The largest earthworm known today is the giant Gippsland. It can grow to a length of 12 feet (3.7 m)!

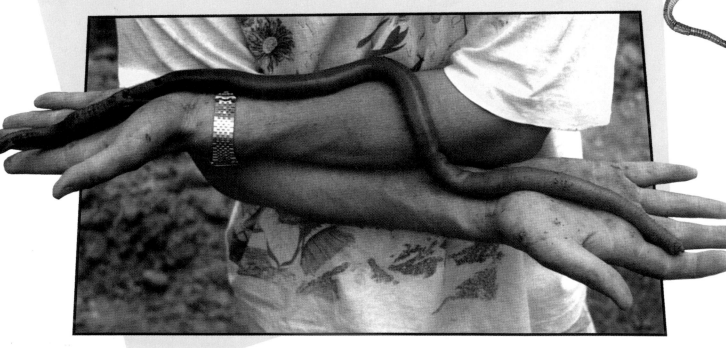

*The giant Gippsland earthworm lives only in Australia. Most species of giant earthworms live in warm climates. They need large spaces in which to **burrow**.*

New to North America

Most of the earthworm species that live in North America today are **introduced species**, or species that were brought to one area from another. Most of these worms arrived in the soil of plants that were brought by early European settlers.

Common species

Two of North America's most common earthworm species—dew-worms and red wigglers—are introduced species. Fully grown dew-worms are three to twelve inches (8-30 cm) long. Fully grown red wigglers are two to four inches (5-10 cm) long.

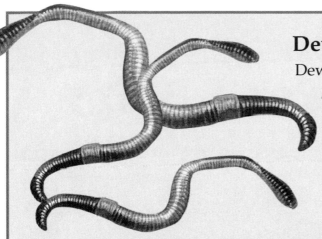

Dew-worms

Dew-worms, also known as night crawlers, are among the largest earthworms in North America. They dig burrows deep into the ground. Dew-worms are big, appetizing meals for **predators**, or animals that eat other animals. Dew-worms are also popular fish bait.

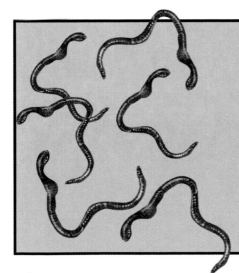
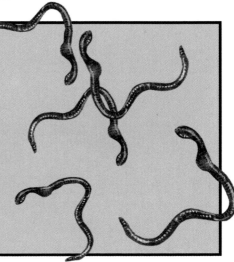

Red wigglers

Red wigglers are small worms. They are also known as manure worms. Red wigglers stay closer to the ground's surface than do dew-worms. They dig groups of tunnels that stretch sideways as well as downward.

AN EARTHWORM'S BODY

Hold on tight!

An earthworm's body has eight setae around each segment. The setae can move in or out. They poke out when the earthworm needs to grip the walls of its tunnels in soil. When the earthworm does not need to grip, it pulls in its setae.

An earthworm's body looks as though it is made up of many rings. The rings are actually body segments—at least one hundred of them! The outside of each segment has tiny bristles called **setae** on it. The setae **grip**, or hold, the soil as the earthworm moves.

Simple senses

An earthworm does not have eyes, ears, or a nose, but it does have a very simple brain. Through its **nerve cells**, it can sense objects, light, and **vibrations**. An earthworm also has nerve cells on its body that help the worm feel its way through soil.

An earthworm's skin is covered with a moist coating. Moisture helps the earthworm breathe through its skin. Earthworms avoid sunlight because the sun dries out their skins.

Inside an earthworm's body

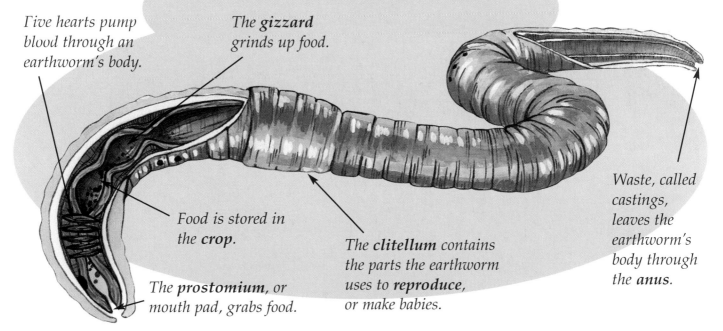

Five hearts pump blood through an earthworm's body.

*The **gizzard** grinds up food.*

*Food is stored in the **crop**.*

*The **prostomium**, or mouth pad, grabs food.*

*The **clitellum** contains the parts the earthworm uses to **reproduce**, or make babies.*

*Waste, called castings, leaves the earthworm's body through the **anus**.*

WHAT IS A LIFE CYCLE?

Every animal goes through a series of **stages**, or changes, called a life cycle. First, it is born or hatches from an egg. The animal then grows and changes until it becomes an adult that can make babies of its own. With each baby, a new life cycle begins. All earthworms go through these changes during their life cycles. Some earthworms move through the stages more quickly than others, however, depending on their **life spans**.

Life span

An animal's life cycle is not the same as its life span. A life span is the length of time an animal is alive. Many earthworms live four to eight years under good conditions—in warm, moist soil with plenty of food to eat.

From egg to earthworm

An earthworm's life cycle starts inside an egg. Earthworm eggs are contained inside a protective case called a **cocoon**. **Hatchlings**, or baby earthworms, wriggle out of the cocoon. The hatchlings dig into the soil right away. They eat a lot as they become **juveniles**, or young earthworms. An earthworm is **mature**, or fully grown, when it develops its **reproductive parts**. It is then ready to **mate**, or join with another adult to make babies. When a mature earthworm lays eggs, a new life cycle begins with each egg.

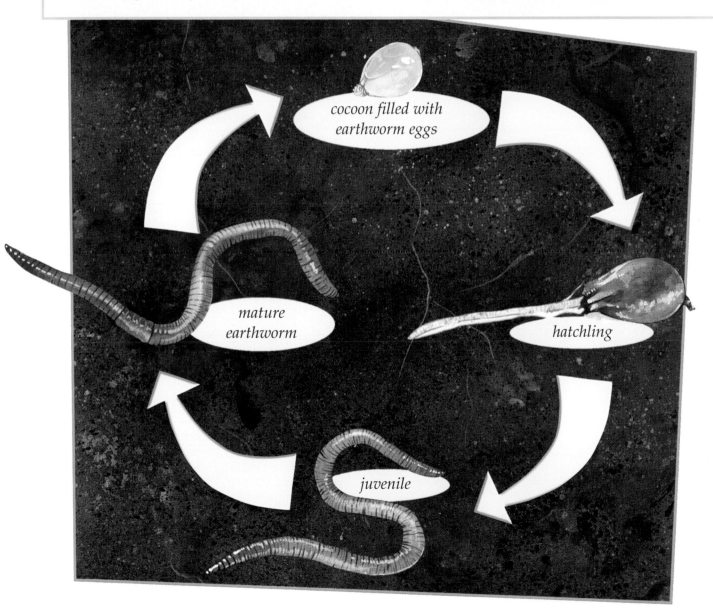

cocoon filled with earthworm eggs

mature earthworm

hatchling

juvenile

INSIDE A COCOON

Earthworms that live in areas with moist, warm climates produce cocoons year round. When the soil is cold or dry, earthworms make fewer cocoons. Each cocoon contains many eggs. It can take weeks or even months for earthworm **embryos**, or developing babies, to form inside the eggs. Every cocoon contains a white sticky substance that provides **nutrients**, or food energy, for the embryos. The embryos use these nutrients as they grow.

Getting bigger

Although each cocoon contains many eggs, only a few embryos develop completely. When the embryos are fully formed, they fill the entire cocoon. The fully developed embryos are then ready to hatch.

An adult earthworm does not stay with its cocoon to protect the embryos inside it.

Fair-weather worms

The length of time it takes an embryo to develop depends on the weather. When the weather is warm and rainy, the soil is warm and moist. Embryos develop quickly in this type of soil. In the spring and the fall, when the soil is wet, most embryos take about three weeks to develop.

Embryos develop more slowly in winter and summer, when the soil is dry.

Out into the world

Hatchlings are white in color and about a half inch (1.3 cm) long. Their bodies are only as thick as pieces of thread.

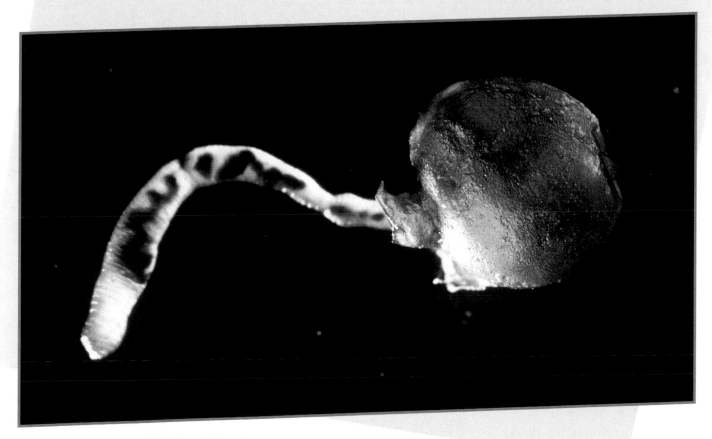

*This hatchling is **transparent**, or see-through. The small dark sections are the hatchling's hearts, crop, gizzard, and **organs**.*

WEE WORMS

A few hours after leaving the cocoon,
a hatchling's skin darkens and changes
color. Hatchlings of different species
turn different colors. Some are pink,
red, or purple, whereas others are
brown, green, blue, gray, or white.
All hatchlings are very slender.

Longer and stronger

Growing earthworms are called juveniles. A juvenile earthworm is smaller than an adult. As it grows, it gets longer and thicker because each of its body segments swells. A few earthworm species grow additional segments as they mature, but most species have the same number of body segments throughout their lives.

It takes between six and 55 weeks for a juvenile earthworm to become an adult. Large species, such as dew-worms, may continue growing and gaining weight for up to one year.

A juvenile earthworm's body does not yet have a clitellum.

BECOMING AN ADULT

An earthworm becomes an adult when its reproductive parts form. The earthworm can then make babies. Most animals develop either male or female reproductive parts, but an earthworm's clitellum contains both male and female parts. The male parts produce **sperm**. The female parts produce eggs.

Depending on the species, an earthworm's clitellum may be white, orangey red, or reddish brown in color.

Ready to mate

An earthworm cannot use its own sperm to **fertilize** its eggs. It must mate with another earthworm. When an earthworm is ready to mate, its clitellum turns orange. The earthworm then finds another earthworm of the same species with which to mate. The two earthworms lie with their clitellums touching and grasp each other using their setae. Their bodies produce slimy coatings that help them stick together. The earthworms then exchange sperm. After mating, both earthworms are able to produce cocoons.

These two adult earthworms are exchanging sperm as they lie close together.

CREATING A COCOON

After two earthworms mate, a thin, sticky covering forms on the outside of each earthworm's clitellum, as shown above. This covering soon forms a cocoon, which will hold the eggs. The earthworm moves backward to slide the covering off its body. As the covering moves along the earthworm's body, the fertilized eggs stick to the covering's inside surface. When the earthworm has wriggled free, the covering closes up and seals itself around the eggs to form a cocoon. The earthworm then moves away from the cocoon, leaving it behind in the soil. An earthworm makes only one cocoon at a time. Before it can make another cocoon, the earthworm must mate again.

Many eggs inside

Each cocoon contains between one and twenty earthworm eggs. Some species of earthworms produce three cocoons per year, whereas others produce 80 cocoons per year. The cocoon is the only protection the eggs have. Many animals, including some types of mites, feed on cocoons.

Have you seen them?

You may have seen earthworm cocoons while digging in a garden or back yard. Cocoons are the size of corn kernels and are shaped like lemons. A new cocoon is yellow and soft. Over time, it darkens to a brown color and becomes much tougher.

More near the top

Species that live near the surface of the soil produce more cocoons than do species that live deep in the soil. Near the surface, the embryos have little protection from the cold and are in danger of freezing. The embryos are also threatened by predators. Making more cocoons ensures that at least some earthworm babies will hatch and start new life cycles.

19

EATING EVERYTHING

Soil contains plants and **microbes**, or tiny animals. It also contains parts of dead plants and animals. An earthworm eats it all! It has no teeth, but it has strong mouth muscles. The earthworm uses its mouth pad, shown below, to take in small pieces of food. It then pulls the food, as well as some soil and small stones, into its mouth. The soil and stones collect in its gizzard, where they help crush and grind up the food.

A dew-worm crawls up to the surface of the soil at night in search of food to pull into its burrow.

Munching away

Earthworms are **decomposers**. Decomposers break down plants and animals in soil by eating and **digesting** them. Both living and dead plants and animals contain nutrients, but earthworms do not use all the nutrients they eat.

Their castings contain the leftover nutrients not used by their bodies. These nutrients become part of the soil and are then used by plants and other animals. The nutrients in castings give plants some of the energy they need in order to grow.

Dew-worms leave piles of castings near the entrances of their burrows.

WATCH OUT, WORM!

The nutrients that earthworms eat are stored in their bodies. These nutrients provide food energy to animals that eat earthworms. Fully grown earthworms have many predators, including snakes, birds, moles, toads, foxes, bears, beetles, centipedes, leeches, slugs, and flatworms. Some predators, such as birds, snatch the earthworms they see above ground, whereas others, such as moles, hunt earthworms underground.

Some people catch earthworms to use as fishing bait!

Knock, knock!

People who gather earthworms sometimes hammer on the surface of the ground to lure earthworms out of their burrows. They know that earthworms head to the surface when they feel the vibrations. The wood turtle, shown below, also makes noises to lure worms to the surface. It stomps its foot or lifts and drops its shell on the ground to make pounding noises.

An earthworm myth

Some people think that if an earthworm is cut in two, it will become two earthworms. This belief is not true! An earthworm can **regenerate**, or regrow, a few segments at its tail end, but it cannot regenerate important parts. In order to regenerate, the front section of the earthworm must contain the clitellum and at least ten segments behind the clitellum. An earthworm could not survive if it were cut in half because it would lose parts of its body that it needed to survive.

The earthworm's newly regenerated segments may be smaller and lighter in color than the rest of its body.

23

TUNNELING THROUGH

An earthworm spends most of its life tunneling through dark soil. As it moves, it mixes together the layers of soil. Blending the soil helps keep it healthy so plants can grow.

Muscles for moving

An earthworm has two types of muscles—circular muscles and long muscles. Circular muscles loop around the earthworm's body inside each segment. Long muscles run from one end of the earthworm's body to the other. To move through soil, the earthworm anchors one end of its body by gripping with its setae. It then uses the circular muscles to stretch out. Finally, the long muscles pull the stretched-out segments closer together.

Heave ho!

As an earthworm moves, it pushes the soil in its path outward. It swallows some soil to create enough space in which to move. As the earthworm passes through the soil, its body leaves **mucus**, or slime, on the tunnel walls. Mucus makes the walls strong so the tunnel can be used again.

Making spaces

Earthworm tunnels make space in the soil for air, water, and the roots of plants. In soil with many earthworm burrows, plant and tree roots are able to grow deeper. Plants with deep roots are healthier than plants with shallow roots.

An earthworm can move forward and backward, but it moves forward more often.

WORMS AND WEATHER

Some worms stay underground for long periods of time, even during heavy rain. They can survive for weeks in soaked soil if there is enough **oxygen** in the water. Oxygen is a gas that is part of the air we breathe. It is also part of water. Earthworms take in oxygen through their skin, either from the air or from water in soil.

Moving on the ground

When it is raining, most species of earthworms move up to the soil's surface in search of food. They can move easily on the wet ground, but many die on the surface, where they are easy targets for all kinds of predators.

Digging deep

Earthworms are most active in the spring and fall, when the soil is moist and the temperature is between 50°F (10°C) and 70°F (21°C). They are not active when the soil is too cold or too dry.

Too hot for worms!

Some earthworms burrow to protect themselves from hot, dry conditions. They enter a period of **estivation**, or inactivity. During estivation, an earthworm curls into a knot. Its skin becomes pale pink.

*An earthworm may enter estivation during a period of **drought**, or little rainfall.*

Brrrr...

An earthworm's body systems slow down in freezing weather to conserve energy. When the temperature drops below freezing, the earthworm **hibernates**, or enters a deep sleep, in its burrow to avoid freezing. If the earthworm freezes, it dies.

THE WORLD'S WORMS

Fortunately, most species of earthworms are thriving all over the world. Without earthworms, the world's soils would not be healthy. Plants that grow in soil with only a few earthworms are not as hardy as plants that grow in soil with plenty of earthworms. However, people need to be aware that many human activities are putting earthworms in danger!

When farmers plow their soil deeply or too often, they may destroy earthworm burrows. Many farmers and gardeners also use **pesticides** on their crops, gardens, and lawns. Pesticides are chemicals that kill insects. Most towns and cities use pesticide sprays in parks and in other open spaces as well. When pesticides are mixed into the soil, they become part of the food earthworms eat and may cause the earthworms to die.

Giant problems

Some earthworm species are **endangered**, or in danger of disappearing from Earth. A few may soon become **extinct**. Extinct animals no longer live anywhere on Earth. The giant earthworm species are at the greatest risk. The Oregon giant has not been seen since 1985, and the giant Palouse earthworm has not been seen since 1978.

Giant species need a lot of space to tunnel and cannot survive when their homes are reduced or eliminated. In both the United States and Australia, the land that is home to giant earthworms is being cleared and used for farming or ranching. Giant earthworms are also harmed by pesticides and **pollution** in the water around farms and ranches.

giant Gippsland earthworm

Worm woes

Worms that live in water, including marine worms, leeches, and other freshwater worms, are also harmed by water pollution. When people dump chemicals into oceans, lakes, rivers, and ponds, many marine animals, including the feather duster worm (shown right) are in danger of dying. The chemicals may eventually soak into the soils nearby and harm earthworm **habitats** as well.

HELPING WORMS

You can help earthworms—and other types of worms, too—by keeping the environment clean. It is important to start in your own back yard, school, and neighborhood. Talk to your teachers, family, and friends about ways to prevent pollution. You can begin by picking up litter in your area. Reducing litter helps keep garbage, which can be harmful to worms, off the ground and out of rivers and lakes.

Mini garbage compactors

You can help reduce the amount of garbage your family produces by using some of it to make **compost**. Compost is decomposing food and plant material. Using earthworms to create compost is called **vermi-composting**. Earthworms such as red wigglers can live in worm bins and eat leftover fruits and vegetables, as well as coffee grounds, pasta, and eggshells. Do not put meat in a compost bin. Feed your earthworms once or twice a week. The castings the earthworms leave behind can then be used on your house or garden plants. They will help plants grow and stay healthy. To learn more, visit http://www.wormdigest.org/buildyourbin.html

Worm watching

If you want to take a closer look at earthworms, all you really need is a shovel. Good places to dig for earthworms are under piles of leaves, in compost heaps, and in gardens. Look for worm castings, which show where earthworms have been. Be careful that you do not hurt the earthworms with your shovel!

Lights out!

Another way to find earthworms is to take a flashlight outside after it rains. Shine the light on the wet grass in your yard or in a park. If you walk softly and shine the light quickly, you may even be able to find an earthworm before it crawls back into the ground.

Learn more

One of the best ways to help earthworms is to learn more about them and the ways in which they help the environment. You can discover more about earthworms by checking out these worm-friendly websites:

- http://yucky.kids.discovery.com/noflash/worm/
- www.urbanext.uiuc.edu/worms/index.html
- www.thegreencommunity.org/giant_worms.html

GLOSSARY

Note: Boldfaced words that are defined in the book may not appear in the glossary.

anus An opening in an animal's body through which waste leaves

burrow (n) An underground tunnel; (v) To make a tunnel underground

climate The longterm weather conditions in an area, including temperature, rainfall, and wind

digest To break down food

fertilize To add sperm to an egg so a baby can form inside

habitat The natural place where a plant or an animal lives

microscope A machine that makes a large image of a tiny object through a lens

nerve cells Special cells on and inside an animal's body that help it sense its surroundings

nutrients A natural substance that helps animals and plants grow

organ A part inside the body that is used for one function, such as digesting food

pollution Harmful materials, such as waste or garbage, which can make the water, air, and soil unclean

reproductive parts The body parts an animal uses to make babies

sperm A male reproductive cell that joins with a female's egg to make babies

vibration A sound created in the ground by movements on the Earth's surface, such as footsteps or rainfall

INDEX

2 3 4 5 6 7 8 9 0   Printed in the U.S.A.   3 2 1 0 9 8 7 6 5